The Su

Clouds

Eleanor Barlow

BookLeaf Publishing
India | USA | UK

Presentation by *BookLeaf Publishing*

Web: www.bookleafpub.com

E-mail: info@bookleafpub.com

ISBN: 9789357446624

First edition 2022

DEDICATION

This poetry book is dedicated to everyone that has inspired me along my journey and who have helped shape me as a person but also have enabled me to grow creatively.

ACKNOWLEDGEMENT

To my friends and family that have supported me on this bumpy journey.

To all the nurses and doctors that have helped me on my journey to recovery.

To my fabulous therapist Enca for believing, encouraging and supporting me on my journey. A massive thank you.

PREFACE

This poetry book is how I endeavour to shine even when I am surrounded by dark clouds. I aim to speak from the heart allowing unfiltered and raw emotions to be expressed on an array of topics. I have also acknowledged some key individuals who have helped me get through this challenging year and have enabled me to get to a better place within myself.

Dad AKA FJ

My father was mad, sad but not a cad
He was a shining knight but not a lad
I loved you so
So why did you have to go

Your love was so true
Even though some of the things you bought
were not shiny or brand new
You had such a warm and gentle heart
It used to make me sad when we had to part

I could not help you
No one could get through
Even your mother tried because you were her
sun
Her star, her moon, her whole life, her little one

But you fell on your sword
Took the rope and tied the cord
I cannot comprehend why you tied the noose
Even though you had stopped the grey goose

But it was too late
All you could here in your mind was hate
It was only when you died

I realised how much I loved you inside

Dad I miss you so
At times it makes me very low
I miss all the fun times we had
Because I do not recall they were all bad

Love you dad, you were my father
A son, a brother, a tree planter
You live on through me
I wish you were alive to see

Sometimes when I look up into the sky
I question God on why you had to die
But that is something I may never understand
I just miss your love and holding your hand

Mum and Dad

My mum is very strong
In her eyes she is rarely wrong

She has a lot to give
But she sprinkles it like a sieve

Her heart is made of solid steal
Because of this we always had a meal

My mother has a lot of knowledge
Even though she stopped education at college

She worked her way to the top
Never allowing the ball to drop

She got married to my gentle giant of a dad
Who was a true gentleman and not a cad

God with all his miracles blessed them thrice
My parents did receive three beautiful mice

The distance between husband and wife grew a part
It makes me question if they got of to a good start

At church there eyes were looking down at the floor
While their minds were not on the sermon but on the back door

The relationship started to decay
The children were the only things in the way

A separation was agreed upon either side
It tore me and my sisters from the inside

My dads life started to dwindle
I tried and failed to the light the fire to rekindle

Yet it was a little too late
He felt like he could not start a new slate

Even though he attended AA
That was not enough to convince him to stay

Death to him seemed the only way
He could not be stopped by anything we would say

Family and friends are still reeling,
I do not think we will ever stop grieving, dealing or healing

His memories, family and work live on
He is still my shinning star even though he has gone

Love you dad you were my shinning knight
You had a beautiful soul that burnt like a candle so bright

My Love Affaire

Oh alcohol I loved you so
You enabled me to escape from life but ultimately left me feeling rather low

It is making me sad that I will not drink you no more
Like what the hell you were my friend and I do not feel ready to close the chapter or even the door

Yes we had a rocky relationship
I knew deep down I had a problem as soon as I had the first sip

Fuck I was in over my head
If it was not for AA then I would have wound up dead

God I really do feel like I have lost an intimate friend
Even though I was in a toxic relationship with alcohol and it was driving me round the bend

Fuck I was so powerless to it

Like at first it was fun and dandy but at times it
got me in real shit

I really do not know what I will do without you
Like how do people cope with losing you?!?
Like I know I need to stop or I will not pull
through

But God all I really want is some of my
favourite cocktails
Even though it was those that sent me off the
rails

God I need you desperately to help cure me
As I am blinded by my addiction which is
preventing me from seeing or being free

I feel bereft that I have not known alcohol that
long
Like is it really that bad that I have a love affaire
with you even though I know it is wrong?!

Sometimes I feel like I have no problem with
alcohol
But I would be lying to you as I need it
desperately to help fill the pain and emptiness
that I feel in my soul

God why is it so easy to have a drink

I really wish I could stop but I cannot and I will just end up projectile vomiting all in the loo or bathroom sink

God I am such an utter mess
And not being able to control this alcoholism pisses me off because I cannot pull it together and it is causing me to stress

It has been a while since I have had a drink in me
I really wish my dad was alive to see

I really am trying here
I am just scared to find out the real person I will become being sober which is causing me anxiety but mostly fear

I know that alcohol is a disease
And I just wish picking up a drink was not as easy as the way I sneeze

God I feel so hopelessly lost
But what I do know is is that I must not go back to alcohol whatever the cost

God I have come to realise alcohol did nothing but harm

Like how could I not see the blaring obvious
signs from my body that acted as an alarm

But alas alcohol had its tenter hooks in me deep
I did try stopping for a while but when I got
enticed back to alcohols loving embrace I felt
home just like being driven by a fancy jeep

Fuck I did not want to end up being an alcoholic
like my dad
But I am one and that just makes me sad

I do not regret the love affaire I had
As it was short but sweet, wrong for me in every
way and just plain bad

All I want to say is that I do not need you
alcohol and that I am joining forces with AA
As they will be my salvation out of this hell I
find myself in and they offer me a way

So fuck you alcohol you are dead to me
I am now closing that chapter or moreover door
to which I am throwing away the key

Alcohol this is my goodbye to you
As you have taken so much and I cannot let you
take my life too

So this is me hanging up my drinking boots
I am now starting to go back and tap into my spiritual roots

God I feel light now for letting this all out and getting it of my chest
At last I feel at peace and now will rest

Chasing The High

God I had an interesting time on it
Actually what the fuck am I talking about it was trippy and left me feeling like shit

Like I was so far gone
I was in the in-between and so lost even with the help of my colleague John

Oh I was stuck in a heavenly place
I was constantly dying over and over again in the same space

No one could understand me
That I was trapped in this utopian world that no one but I could see

It is kind of funny but I did not want to escape
As in that world I was in I was out of pain and could forget about the painful rape

I felt like I was trapped in a snow globe
But it was my safe haven until I was shaken and no longer wanting to wear my fine robe

God it was an experience to have had

Which I am rather thankful for as it was kind of fun and not at all bad

I am not sure how I feel about weed
As after all it is only a plant that grew from a mighty seed

I do not feel that taking weed is all that bad and I believe there is actually some good
But I will be honest I know shit all about weed and could not argue its case as my arguments would be flimsy like plywood

I used to think that a bipolar and weed high were the same
God how thick am I, I seriously know nothing and God I really am lame

There really is a big difference you know
And God how naïve I was it was like I was a person who had never seen snow

Bipolar is a chemical imbalance already in my brain and taking weed is just adding a chemical to my already addled brain
So when I went on it I reached a high that took me to the brink of death and temporarily made me go insane

Like I really do not need that
As I lose touch with reality without needing anything and if I am honest I am nuttier than Alice in Wonderland's cat

When I was on my trip I was in a heavenly place that was so light
I felt so much love that it made me cry as I found acceptance and I did not want to leave even though I had no sight

God my friends kept me grounded and stopped me from floating up
They held me tight even though I wanted to be free and sipping from the eternal cup

The downside of the weed was I was sick everywhere
Like I can never have a GBK milkshake ever again or even go there

God it was a river of white
Like in my mind it was me suffering for everyone's sins and god it was a terrible sight

Like no one but me could understand or see
That I was dying for everyone in the world so that they could all be free

God I kept dying even after I had left
It was killing me inside all the pain that I could feel it was breaking me, leaving me empty and bereft

It really was one hell of an experience of mine
But I survived it, can reflect back on it and I am doing just fine

Weed brought me to a place I want to get back to
It was heaven, somewhere I belonged and I do not want to fight no more as I really did not want to come back or pull through

God I want to take it once more
As I was in heaven not just waiting at the door

God I had found peace and a warmth so deep
I just want to get back to paradise which I will run, jump and make the final leap

God why do I crave weed so bad
It is the feeling I got although scary it took me out of myself to a place I was not afraid to be mad but in fact was rather glad

I know I took way to much
But it relaxed me and freed me from my prison like hutch

Alas I will taste you no more
And just thinking about that is making my heart ache because it is so sad and sore

Goodbye weed my dear friend
It was a laugh, a tad scary but mostly great I just wish you did not drive me round the bend!

Faith What Faith?!?

I am starting to feel a little lost
Like is it really worth it believing in God whatever the cost

Like did Jesus really die for me
As he died a long time ago apparently so that I could be free

Free of what though?
I am a nobody and just thinking like that makes me feel low

Like why should I be saved
As all I have done is just misbehaved

God I so desperately want to be sipping from the eternal cup
But I cannot see how that can be as I am just a young, foolish and naughty little pup

I have been and entered heaven once or twice before
Not just waiting rather impatiently at the door

I am a true sinner

And in life I believe that I am actually a winner

Because I have done, seen and been through so much
That the burden I carry would be too much for anyone to hold even if it was disguised in a glitzy clutch

Like I really am starting to question what I truly believe in
And the stress and pressure I am putting myself under is causing my head to spin

Like who is this omnipotent God
All I know is that Moses had this all powerful staff or wait was it a rod?!?

There is so much pain and destruction
Like I feel we all need a guide or moreover some instruction

Please God I need you
And a part of me knows you need me too

I feel this is a very unbalanced equation
And sometimes I feel you purposely put me in a very difficult situation

I sometimes feel like a puppet on strings

Because sometimes I feel like I have no control
over my life to choose who I meet, see or even
who rings

God I am so confused dot com
And all I want to do is marry this guy called
Tom

Actually I am lying to you there is this special
girl
Who I am head over heals for that I would share
my last Cadbury twirl

Like in the bible I know it says that kind of love
is wrong
But how can I fight these feelings that I have
which are so strong

Surely it cannot be that wrong if one of the
commandments says 'thou shalt love thy
neighbor as thyself'
Like surely being with someone you love is
good for your health?

Like love is just love
Is it not?!? With its feeling leaving you soaring
and flying high like a dove

I believe that there is a heaven and a hell

Well at least I think I do?! Let's take a rain
check on that whilst I quickly answer the bell

Sometimes I feel all alone
And that is true whatever the time zone

Like why is there all this suffering
It is as if I am watching a movie that is still
buffering

Like I know why there are rainbows in the sky
It is because it is your promise not to flood the
earth again and cause humanity to die

I really do not understand you God
Sometimes I think you are a real bastard or
moreover a cruel sod

Like they say Gods timing
But it's not mine which I find hugely frustrating
and I cannot help the fact that I wake up
rhyming

There are so many religions out there
Like how do I know which one to follow it is not
as simple as choosing a pear

So where do I start

Is faith something that you feel in your soul or with your heart?

What I do know and believe is that there is a God out there
Which I guess is a pretty good foundation to have like having loose change to spare

But why God is there so much injustice to be had?!?
Because I cannot cope with it as I feel so much and it just makes me sad

I want to save the world like how Jesus tired to heal the sick
Yet I am being stonewalled mostly by men who are leading our countries into ruin by operating and thinking with their dick

God we are all your lost little sheep
That desperately need your support, guidance and also some much needed sleep

We have all fallen from grace
And on a planet that has been created and flung into space

You made us from dust
And in the big book teach us not to lust

But we are only human after all
And lust is what we all do and that is why we had to fall

And fall we did do
Which I know truly hurt you

That is why we need to pray
To ask for forgiveness, to have someone to be accountable for our actions and for what we say

God I do not feel that I am enough
And because of these feelings I constantly surround myself with materialistic people and stuff

The world is such a beautiful place
But people are too busy to stop and take stock as they are too focused on their own race

The race is what we call life
And some people are only concerned with finding a husband or wife

Life is a wonderful journey to be on
And before you know it it can be taken from you and you will be all gone

It says no sex before marriage which just blows my mind
Like that rule is surly unnatural for mankind

Like do people actually follow that backward teaching
Because for me it is a topic that pastors are constantly preaching

Sometimes all I want to do is be in the baby blue sky
Like why did I fail in my attempt to die?

I know that God has a plan for me
I just wish I was given a sneak preview and allowed to see

They say that God is three in one
But sometimes all I feel is that he is just around to steal my fun

I feel that god is all around us
And I know that when I reach heaven that there will be an almighty fuss

And all I want is to feel accepted by the man (or woman) above me
And grow old and wise like that of an oak tree

Like who says God has to be a man?!?
Oh actually God probably is, as man was made first and then Eve came along to endure him for her entire life span!

God why is the world filled with so much hate
Like we must be on this earth for a reason other than finding a mate who will probably show up late

The world is filled with so much crime
And is it really worth killing and dying to get a pretty dime

He turned water into wine you know
And girl I wish I enjoyed it as it would make me feel better similar to eating raw cookie dough

God I feel your love for me which is so deep
I just wish I did not have this desire to die and take the final leap

Oh why God does life have to be so hard
It sometimes feels like I am having to walk through lard

Sometimes life can be a real bore
And for some actually having to work each day seems like a real chore

But I actually live to work as it makes me feel and come alive
And this is because I love what I do and I do it for lots of reasons not just to survive

Oh why do people have to leave us behind and die
As all it does is cause me so much anguish, sadness and grief that I just want to cry

I lost my dad to suicide and my question is where were you??
He needed you desperately but you were not there for him and he was not able to pull through

God you have failed me
Or maybe that is just my anger blinding me from being able to see

But I do not care no more
As a big part of me feels that you walked out the front door

A very long time ago when I was a kid
Like you saw how scared, lonely and lost I was to the point that I hid

I hid from you and in turn lost my way

And I have been clawing my way back to you
each and every day

Sometimes it is easier to just say that I am
spiritual
Rather than follow a particular faith or ritual

Sometimes I find that I do not know where I
stand
Like I need you God to hold me tight and lead
me gently by the hand

I know that the bible holds a lot of wisdom and
truth
Even though most of the books are recorded by
men there are a few womanly accounts and
characters like that of dear Ruth

I know that I am special in Gods eyes
I just wish I could believe it and ignore all the
negative pollution that comes from the media's
lies

I am glad and thankful that I believe in
something
And when I am in church I feel light as a feather
because I am able to praise, worship and sing

I just wish I could figure out and analyse Gods mind
As I am sure it would be a real treasure trove and something great to find

I will finish with some gratitude
And that is thanking god for loving me unconditionally and never giving me back any attitude

Violated

I was taken advantage of by the first ever man
And this is something I have not really disclosed
to many because it is too painful like being
burned by oil from a frying pan

I am just going to say it
I got burned real hard and I truly got bit

It is only now I feel ready to share my deep,
dirty and shameful secret...I am a victim of rape
Just saying that leaves a bitter, sour nasty taste in
my mouth like that of a grape

I am struggling to cope
I have lost my mind and I am struggling to see
or find hope

It happened a couple of years back
And the experience has left me feeling discarded
like a potato sack

I need to come to terms with what has happened
to me

And even though I have made peace with the ordeal I went through I still feel chained and not free

God please erase my pain
I feel like I have learned the lesson and there is now nothing left to gain

I felt used and unwanted like the offcuts and cheap pieces of meat
After the rape I was struggling to focus and sit still on the train seat

He just drilled himself into me
I was in agony but no one could see

He stuck it in
So hard and fast that my head started to spin

I hold my hands up high
As I feel I am partly to blame and that's what makes me want to die

I agreed to the first part
But then he flipped me over and took me from behind and tore me apart

He used no protection with me

I felt like a little fuck toy and that was all I was
for him and what I needed to be

I was and he was partly of our faces
He was rough and put me through his paces

God I feel so violated inside
I feel so angry with myself and just want to run
and hide

I don't thing I can ever have sex
Because he fucked me so hard like that of an
extinct t-rex

I just needed to get this pain off my chest
And I am now at peace and I can rest.

Ma Petite Mademoiselle

Oh my dear sweet Suchita
You really are my beautiful senorita

You have such a heart of gold
And you are like my baby sis as you are only
twenty years old

God you are one powerful pocket rocket
As you light up the ward like a lamp when
plugged into a socket

I really am sorry that I gave you a fright
That was wrong of me and not right

Because you are a true princess to the core
And without you life is a real bore

You always make me laugh
And I love how you have made the bold choice
not to wear a headscarf

And girl you look so fine in your sari

And if I had one I would take you around in my
Ferrari

And you have such a beautiful smile
With a personality to match and bags of style

And I really am going to miss you
Because you have supported me and seen me
through

And I am so bereft that we have to part
Because you have really captured a piece of my
heart

And I wish you well at university, which you
will ace
As you are intelligent and not just a pretty face

Just remember you are a Stella
And with you I would dance the tarantella

As you shine so bright
Like a star in the night

So arrivederci my love
And spread your wings like a dove

Mills

My dearest, darling and gorgeous mills
When you get angry it has me running for the
hills
Because you really do have a look that kills

Like you have a stair that leaves its mark
But also a smile that banishes away the dark
With a voice that sounds sweeter than a lark

Like I do not know how I would have coped
without you
And I really cannot apologise enough for
breaking a chair or two
Like I probably should have just talked things
through

Yes, I know it has been a bumpy ride
And I have hated all the rules that I have had to
abide
But you must know that I am on your side

Because I really do care for you very much
As you have been my lifeline, my crutch
During the dark days where I have felt like a
prisoner cooped up in a small hutch

And I am going to miss you when it is time to
say goodbye
But I am ready to go as I am no longer high
And I no longer have thoughts or feelings of
wanting to die

Miss you long time
And thank you for being with me on my journey
or moreover my climb.
Back to recovery to the point where life now
feels sublime

Needing You

God I have reached the destination of insanity
And I also sometimes rely on my vanity

Oh no one understands the place I went to
I really pray you can help me otherwise I cannot see a way through

There is a little piece of me that is forever lost
But I am willing to do whatever it takes no matter the cost

To help me work through my issues
Which I know will have you bringing out the tissues

I know you will endeavour to do your best
But I feel I am too far gone and all I want to do is be laid to rest

Oh God why am I such a lost soul?
I am tumbling and falling down my own manmade hole

I really do need your help

But like a dog I cannot speak but only cry and
yelp

I am such a basket case
And sometimes I feel like I am wasting your
time and precious headspace

Like why do you want to help someone like me?
Like I really cannot see all that you see

Like I have fallen so far from grace
And I feel I cannot argue my case

Of why I desperately need you
In my life as I am struggling to cope with feeling
so blue

Ah I really am a mess
And I cannot see myself being of any use which
is causing me to stress

My broken brain lies in pieces on the ground
And I have reached a point where I do not want
to be around

At the start of the session I was scared to open
up all the way
Because a part of me was terrified of what you
were going to say

Yet after our first session I was sold
As you really are fantastic and worth your weight in gold

And I hate how our sessions go by so quick
Because they are enjoyable as we can have a laugh and at times can take the mick

I hope in time you will be able to understand my fragile mind
As you are knowledgeable, wise and your words are kind

I really am asking for a miracle here
And I am thankful for you as I am starting to heal and that is down to you my dear

God I am starting to love therapy very much
As it is helping get me out of my prison like hutch

I feel that I am growing each and everyday
And it made me sad that we had to stop sessions in May

Like I really could not cope
With not talking to you and I got to a dark place where I started to lose hope

In me ever getting well
And all I did in hospital was sit and dwell

On how I had lost you
And that really tore me in two

Because I felt that we had formed a connection
And with you I could start to work on all the feelings of rejection

Which I experienced as a child
Which may explain why I can be so wild

Like I really feel you are good for me
And after each session I feel light and free

And I cherish the two slots of time I have with you
As I feel so much better for talking things through

I really am blessed that Candy gave you my number
As I was struggling with a deep depression that was causing me to slumber

And I love that we can talk a while
And how we can hear each other smile

Whenever we speak
That it makes me look forward to your phone calls each week

You have such a soothing voice
And you will always be my first choice

When it comes to someone I turn to
As you yourself have pulled through

Like you understand me on my dark days
And know how to help me address my destructive ways

I really feel you are going to be my lifeline
And with your support and guidance I believe I will be just fine

Emmanuella

God you really are a true Sinderella
That I would cast you as the main protagonist in my new novella
And I really do need you desperately in my life Emmanuella
To the point that I wish I could replace your fella
As I know I am better and would hold your umbrella

And you have a body to die for
To the point that I love watching you Waltz out the door
And I love the way you express yourself because it is real and raw
And I feel that you are a woman that is loyal to the core

I really love that I made you run
So girl please do some cardio with me as I know you will have fun
And what I love is that your personality shines brighter than the sun

And girl you are a real stunner
Even though you are not a runner

And you really are a jewel in the NHS

A real diamond so rare to find
And you really are one of a kind
With features that are clearly defined
And one of God's creations so beautifully designed
But what I need is you to get me out of hospital before I lose my mind

And I actually like it when we have our little disagreements and fights
As it is kind of fun and takes our relationship to new heights
And you know I would stick up for you and your rights
And with you I just want to turn on all the lights

To keep the darkness at bay
Until the next day
When the sun will rise with its powerful ray

Like you have a beautiful soul
That when I am with you it helps fill my enormous man made sized hole

And God you really are sassy

That you would fit right in on MTV
But what you want is the latest Louis V
And girl you are the real deal, the D&G
With a spirit that is so wild and free
And you really do mean the world to me

Which is why I will always be on your side
And I love it how you make me blush so that I run and hide
And yes our relationship has been one hell of a bumpy ride
But I will come through for you and provide

Because you have captured a piece of my heart
And I will admit that I liked you from the start
And it is really making me sad that we will have to part

So please remember that you are enough
And you really don't need all that materialistic stuff!

As you are a true beauty Queen

Who has such a stunning complexion
That you mirror that of the beautiful Cinderella's reflection
And girl you are pure perfection
And with you I have a deep connection

Which is why I am offering you my protection

Because I can look after you as I am a bit of a lad
And you know you can share my bachelor pad
But what I really hate is when we fight and you get mad
As it huts me and leaves me feeling sad

But we always kiss and make up
Which makes me happy because I am one excitable and loveable pup
And with you I would share my last Reese's Peanut Cup

Because you are a shimmering, shinning star
And you are so special and will go far

So Keep Dreaming, Loving and Laughing

Falling For You

God I am falling, falling so deep
Into your eyes that I just want to keep

Forever and a day as they are so seductive
And with you by my side we can be so
productive

In all that we do
And what I need to know is if you like me too

Because I have fallen from grace
And you are all that occupies my headspace

God I am really struck
By your inner and outer beauty that I need a fire
truck

To cool down the feelings I have for you
And the energy we create which I know you can
feel too

And you are more precious to me than platinum
or gold
And I would never leave you hanging or put you
on hold

As you are my number one and deserve to come first
And with me I will always quench your thirst

Because girl you really have got me all smitten
With you as you are adorable like that of a baby kitten

I want you to know that you will always be enough
And with you I want to build a life and share all my stuff

Because you are a star for me that shines so bright
With a beautiful smile that is a wondrous sight

With you I want to take off into the night sky
Where we would be free to fly high

And God I do not know if this is love
But I feel such peace like when I saw that white dove

It has been a long time since I have felt this way
About anyone, I must say

And I really do feel something stirring in my heart
And I feel sad when we have to part

Because you cheer me up
And I just act like an excited pup

When I get to see you
Because you see me through and through

That is for the real me
And I cannot wait until I am free

From my prison that I find myself in
And I know loving you is actually a sin

But I do not care
If people talk or stare

So please give me a chance to love you
Because that is something you deserve and what I want to do

But what do you actually want
Because if it is me then I know the best cafe for a croissant

I hope in time you will be mine

Because with you by my side I know I will be just fine

My Fairy Godmother

God you mean the world to me
You have helped me to see
How wonderful the world can be

Your heart is so pure and true
And I have always felt deeply loved by you
As you have helped me so much and seen me pull through

And you have been there for me through thick and thin
And have helped me stay grounded when my head would spin
And you have always rooted for me to win

In life and in everything that I do
Which is why you are not just my godmother but my friend too
And I really do not know what I would do without you

Because you have been by my side

And have always offered me a ride
But more importantly you have never lied

To me at all
And you are always someone I can call
And have been there to catch me when I would fall

You really do hold a special place in my heart
And I love spending time with you as you have so much wisdom to impart
As well as all the galleries we go to, to admire the fine art

You truly are heaven sent
And you always make my birthday a special event
And from you I have learned the importance of why we repent

And you will forever be my shooting star
And I cannot thank you enough for taking me to Durham in your car
Which I know was very far

You have always stuck up for me and my rights
And helped defuse our family fights
And I love that we both share a fear of heights

And what I love is getting to walk Harry your dog
Because we go to Richmond Park and get to enjoy a coffee whilst sitting on a log
And I love how your favourite animal is a frog

And your personality shines so bright like the sun
And with you I always have so much fun
And my love for you is greater than a tonne

My Body And I

I wish I felt pretty
But most of the time I feel shitty

As I do not feel I have a beautiful complexion
And I hate passing mirrors as they show my reflection

I really struggle to accept my dress size
So I wear baggy clothes that act as a disguise

I just want to be comfortable in my own skin
But I am all consumed by wanting to be thin

Like I am onto my next fad
Yet it will just fail and leave me feeling sad

Like I have tried them all
But I end up hitting a brick wall

Like why do I do this to myself?
Like a big part of me knows it is bad for my health

But I am blinded by my quest
For perfection and I will not rest

Until I have a body to die for
Which will leave me skipping happily out the front door

I get that there is so much more to me
But my body is the first thing that people see

So I want it looking great
So I can feel comfortable when I date

Like all I want is my body to be toned and strong
Like is that really so wrong?

Like I wish I could accept me for me
But I cannot and I just compare myself to the people that I see

Mixed Episode

God I was falling, spiralling down
Into a depression
That was causing me to frown

At times I was soaring up in the sky
Yet I was stuck in a loop
Forever chasing the high

I found myself frozen in space and time
To my childhood days
That were far from sublime

I was no longer able to show my face
As I was so embarrassed
Because I had fallen far from grace

And I had lost control over my life
In fact I was in prison
Surrounded by nothing but strife

A part of me inside was slowly dying
But no one could see
As I was concealing all my crying

And I was stuck in a perpetual cycle of pain

Which I had no control over
Because my heart just poured with rain

Abuse

Screaming, shouting cursing,
The abuse kept on bursting

Whack...
Smack...

The beatings did come
Until I could no longer feel my bum

It went one, two, three
Until I could barely see

And this abuse went on for years
Whilst inside I was drowning from all my tears

And like an onion I did shed
My little heart into pieces till it turned to led

You told me that you loved me
But enslaved I was not able to be free

You never gave me my adult wings to fly
So I never matured or learned how to navigate
the sky

I turned 18 but that was just a number
It meant very little so I stooped into a slumber

I love you even still
And I keep your picture on my window sill

Yet abuse is all that I have come to know
Like you have a kind heart but you do not let it
show

A materialistic love you gave
And now you have lost me because it is just a
little too late to save

I have been locked away in this cage too long
And I am getting tired of singing the same old
sad little song

I think some time apart is needed right now
As otherwise I may attempt to exit and take the
final bow

The passing down of generational trauma and
abuse
Has played a role in my drug and alcohol misuse

And do not get me started on the genetics that
were passed down

Like I might as well run away to the circus and
become a clown

And you know I really did try to be strong
But all I did was constantly put a foot wrong

Being the eldest came with a lot of responsibility
And I often struggled believing in my academic
ability

Oh why is life so hard
Like my childhood has left me feeling rather
scarred

I hope in time we can talk things through
As I really have so much to say to you

And may God be in our favour I pray
So that we know what words to say

C3

God I really do love my coffee
And here at C3 you can get creative making a funky tie-dye tee
And you will leave the cafe feeling inspired and free
And I hope you can all see the vision for C3

As you are going to love it in here
As you will get quality in more ways than one and the price will not be too dear
The cafe will also leave your head, heart, mind feeling light and clear
And it will be a place where you will find acceptance and no need to shed a tear

What you will find is a hard-working, dedicated and passionate team
And I hope with your support we can make this a reality and not just a dream
Here in the cafe you will get your tea, scones, jam and clotted cream
And it will be a hub of activity where we help build your self-esteem

Here at C3 we will become so successful that we will win numerous awards
And that is something I want for us as a team to aim towards
You will see that here at C3 we will set and break all the records
And in the cafe we will host a number of crafts, activities and have a variety of game boards

But more importantly I want the cafe to be a place to relax, rejuvenate and regroup
And I am sure you will love the house special soup
We are a small team built on respect, understanding and we are a solid troop
You will feel the love, warmth and dedication which we aim to give whilst keeping you up to date and in the loop

You will be in a safe environment that will act as a protective bubble
As we will rebuild from the ground up out of the rubble
And in the cafe if you wish you can get a double
Of whatever you want without no judgement or fear of getting into any trouble

Here at C3 you will have meaningful employment and a sense of purpose in your life

You may even end up bagging a husband or even a wife
At C3 you will find no cause for strife
And we will always be here to help with anything like cutting your toast into soldiers with a knife

If you want the best coffee in town then come to us
As you will find a chilled atmosphere and no fuss
Our foundation is built on respect, trust and helping reduce the need to cuss
And our coffee will be out of this world that you will make the trek to us whether that be by train, car or bus

Worry

God I am worried about you right down to my core
And the last thing I want to see is you walk back through the hospital door

I am whirling, swirling and tumbling down
Because you are making me sad that I am wearing a huge frown

What can I say or do
To get through to you

Because you have me worried sick
And I do not like your boyfriend as I think he is a prick

You need to stop taking cocaine
Before it drives you insane

You know I am just a phone call away
So please go home and listen to what I have to say

As I do not want you to die

Because you are way to precious and young to
be in the heavenly sky

You are amazing you know
And me not being able to help you is making me
very low

God I really am scared for you
And I am starting to fear that you will not pull
through

Like for fucks sake you got hit
And I am worried that you are going to overdose
and have a fit

Please listen to your friends
Because we care about you and what you are
doing is driving us around the bends

I really am scared I am going to lose you
And a lot of people are also worried too

You only have the one life
And you are way too young to have it snuffed
out with the blade of a knife

Please come back to us
Because we care so much about you that we
would travel by train, car or bus

To get to you
So that we can pull you through

Out of the shit you are in
Before you go loopy and your head starts to spin

Love you long time
And please be careful as you are too sublime

For this world to lose
As you are a ray of sunshine that help banish away the blues

And you know I have really struggled to sleep
Because I was so concerned on how far you have fallen into the deep

Quagmire of destruction
Where all I can do is give you my advice and instruction

So please come back, as I miss you so much
And all I want to do is help you out of your prison like hutch!

Food

God I am so addicted
If gluttony was a crime then I would be
convicted

I wish I did not enjoy the naughty stuff
But I do and I just cannot seem to get enough

Sugar is the real killer for me
Even the healthy kind that comes from a tree

As I just want more and more
Until I am cradling my stomach on the bathroom
floor

I wish I did not struggle with food
But sometimes it is the only thing that lifts my
mood

Food has the power to make me happy
Especially when I am feeling rather crappy

Like I love sugar so much
As it is my friend, my crutch

But it is eating me alive

So I need to be careful if I want to survive

Or I will end up in a bad way
Where my body stops functioning or listening to what my brain has to say

Like sometimes I eat well
And it leaves me feeling pretty swell

But at other times I eat to excess
Which just causes my body to stress

As it cannot cope
Especially when I consume too much dope

Like I struggle to find a balance when I eat
As I seem to always crave something sweet

Food has such a hold over me
I often feel enslaved to it and not free

Like I do not understand why I struggle so bad
Like when I fall off the healthy bandwagon I just get mad

Because all I need is to build in some healthy habits
Rather than munching down on Lindt bunny rabbits

N.O.

Where to start?
You have such a beautiful and kind heart

Like I really do not know what I would do
without you
As you have seen me when I am high but also
when I am blue

Like you really have left your mark on me
Which I think it is evident for all to see

I love that you understand my crazy fruit loop
mind
And with you around I find it easy to unwind

As your energy is calm and warm
And with you I know we can wether any storm

You have such an angelic face
That I feel you are heaven sent as you have such
ethereal grace

I wish you were here more
Because without you life in hospital is a real
bore

You are stunning both inside and out
And that is something I hope you will never doubt

I want you to know that I care deeply for you
But you have one fatal flaw which is not loving chocolate as much as I do!

But I can work with that because I think you are swell
And I feel I am starting to get to know you very well

And that is something I feel in my bones
And I would love to take you to the beach to collect shells and skip stones

Like you really are a beautiful butterfly
And with you I want to soar high into the night sky

You have such a beautiful spirit inside
And I wish we did not have to hide

The fact that you make my heart skip a beat
And with you around I feel complete

Like we really would make an unstoppable force

And together we could take on any course

Like I can see us remaining good friends
As together we can drive each other round the curves and bends

You are soft to the touch
And God I have fallen hard and I really like you very much

And what I feel for you is a real life attraction
Which is not just a physical or chemical reaction

But something I feel when I am around you
And I know you can feel it too

So let me show you what real love can feel like and be
Because I can make you feel safe, loved
and looked after better than Bruce Lee

Made In Chelsie

If I am North and you are West
Then together we will find the treasure chest
Because when we work together we are the best

And you really are a wonderful free spirit
Who enjoys working at festivals because it is fun and allows you a free ticket
And I think you are sexier than that of the infamous Bridget

And I wish I could take you out as I know we would have a ball
Because I would be there to catch you if you would fall
And girl I would be at your beck and call

But scrap that as that is way too needy
Like all I want is to be your running partner because I bet you are speedy
And that would mean more time with you which I want as I am rather greedy

Well actually it is because I like you
And I know you enjoy my company too
And I think it is cool that you enjoy what you do

Like you have gorgeous sea blue eyes
That I get lost in as with them I see truth and no lies
And I really am going to be sad when I have to say my goodbyes

Like when I was admitted I was rather shy
And at times I just wanted to die
But you were always there and became my close ally

And I loved making you jump
Because with you I never got the hump
And you always managed to get me out of a slump

And what I really love are your neon running shorts
Because it is clear to all that you love your sports
And I bet you would thrash me if we were to play on the tennis courts

I really feel like I am starting to know you well
And you know you have me under your spell
Because you have helped me up and out of my internal prison like hell

And I love that your favourite chocolate bar
Is dark chocolate which is the healthiest by far
And to me what you are is a magic star

Suicide

My father lost his life to suicide
He had reached a dark place that he could no
longer hide

He made the decision
He was tired of being stuck in his internal prison

He prepared the rope
He had lost all sight of hope

The noose was all ready
His mind, body and spirit were steady

He put his neck in the noose
Stepped off the chair that was loose

He no longer cared as his spirit would be set free
His body writhed and twisted until he could no
longer see

It was a sad sight as he was not that very old
And as a giant it must have been a sight to
behold

The tree just stood tall and looked on

While his family and friends weeped because he was gone

The light of his life had flickered out
And when I found out I just wanted to shout

I had tears in my eyes
How could he do this to our lives

Anger, sorrow and grief
Took over my life like a ninja thief

My world was starting to fall a part
Yet this was only just the start

As suicide is something hard to deal
As it leaves a wound that will never heal

But the memory's live on as they are real
And that is something no one can ever steal

Milton Keynes UK
Ingram Content Group UK Ltd.
UKHW020712090824
446757UK00011B/705

9 789357 446624